To Mom
with love
David and Ginny
Kids

Golden prayers

Golden Prayers

Compiled by Jo Petty

The C.R. Gibson Company, Norwalk, Connecticut

INTRODUCTION

When the disciples asked Jesus to teach them to pray, the Lord's response was a prayer that was simple and unpretentious yet so beautiful that it has endured as the most beloved devotion of Christians through the centuries. Truly the Master's words were "fitly spoken."

It is my belief that our prayers—like the Lord's—need not be expressed in flowery, fancy language. Nor does God ask us to fall on our knees or visit a church to pray. Rather, He wants us to be ourselves, to create a quiet place within for Him and to make a habit of speaking to Him, in our own style, as we go about the earthly work He has given us to do.

My own prayers have always been simple conversations with my Best Friend. In this book, I have shared these with you, my faithful readers. Some are my adaptations—or simplifications—of familiar writings from Scripture, the Hymnal and other great Christian writings, others came to me spontaneously both in times of trial and triumph. I offer this personal prayer book in the hope that it will serve to guide and comfort others as much as it has me throughout my life.

Jo Petty

Lord,
have mercy

Give us thankful hearts for all Your mercies. There is a wideness in Your mercy like the wideness of the sea!

May our hearts be filled with mercies, kind- ness, humility, meekness; may we forbear one another and forgive one another.

O God, I will sing of Your power; I will sing aloud of Your mercy in the morning.

You have shown us what is good and what You require of us.

When we think of Your mercies, Father, we are lost in wonder, love and praise.

The earth is full of Your mercy!

Our transgressions are forgiven and our sins are covered.

We bless You, O God, for You have not turned away our prayers.

Create in me a clean heart, O God, and renew a right spirit within me.

Let us come boldly to You,
    that we may obtain mercy and grace that
    will help us in time of need.

Satisfy us early with Your mercy, so that
    we may be glad.

Save us for Your mercy's sake.

May we keep ourselves in Your love, looking for
    the mercy of our Lord Jesus Christ.

As the heaven is high above the earth, so
    great is Your mercy toward those who fear You.

Thank You for forgiving the sins of all
    who are penitent.

Therefore have we hope.

All Your paths, Lord, are mercy and truth.

I will sing unto You, for You have dealt bountifully
with me.

You heal all our diseases; You redeem our life
from destruction; You crown us with
loving-kindness and tender mercies.

We trusted in Your mercy, Lord, and
our hearts rejoice in Your salvation.

You are full of compassion.

Show me Your ways. Teach me Your paths.

Our smallest sin should humble us. But
because of Your mercy we must not despair
of our greatest sin.

Hear us and have mercy on us.

Help us to forgive.

Your tender mercies are over all Your works.

Let Your mercies come, O Lord.

Jesus said, Blessed are the merciful, for
   they shall obtain mercy. Help me to be
   merciful.

I will rejoice in Your mercy,
   for You have considered my trouble.

May I always show mercy with cheerfulness.

Surely goodness and mercy shall follow
   me all the days of my life,
   and I shall dwell in Your house forever.

Dear Jesus,
   May we know You more clearly,
   May we love You more dearly,
   May we follow You more nearly.

Lord, teach us love

Father, lead me in the more excellent way—Love.

You gave Your only begotten Son, so that whosoever believes in Him should not perish, but have everlasting life!

Each day may we remember that every good gift and every perfect gift is from You.

Help us to live this day in love of You and in obedience to Your holy will.

May we have a continual sense of Your abiding presence.

May we daily become more and more like Jesus.

Thank You for Your love.

Thank You for supplying all of our needs.

Thank You for the angels that You
    send to minister for us.

Thank You for making it simple enough
    for us to understand that we should believe
    in Jesus Christ, and love one another.

Father, You have made men to dwell
    on the face of the earth. Help us
    to live as brothers.

May we so love You that we may give love to
    others.

Remind us that every deed of love we
    do to another is done to You.

Give us grace to love our neighbors
    as ourselves.

Make us quick to see the needs
    of those less fortunate than ourselves.

May we always have care for one another,
knowing that as when one member of our body
suffers, all of the members suffer with it.

Give us Your love, which will make us
care one for another.

Never let us forget the poor, or those
sick or in prison or hungry or thirsty.

Thank You, Father, for the knowledge that
we have passed from death unto
life because we love our brothers.

May we please our neighbors rather
than ourselves.

May we try to understand rather than
seek to be understood.

Increase our love so that our spirit
of forgiveness will increase.

Give us the power to forgive all who
have trespassed against us, so that we may be
forgiven our trespasses against You.

Forgive us our sins.

Help me to love those who do not love me
and to be good to those who are
not good to me.

Help me to love my enemies.

Help me to give without counting the cost.

Help me to labor without asking for
any reward.

May I learn to forgive quickly as
little children do.

Forgive us, Lord, for we have never loved
anybody enough—not even our families
and friends. How could we love our enemies?

Forgive our lack of love.

Our love is weak—we love only those
who love us.

If we have not loved the stranger, forgive.

May we always remember others in our prayers.

Teach us that our prayers can bring
blessings to others.

May we set our affections on things above
rather than on things on the earth.

May we be grateful for our material pos-
sessions yet not set our hearts upon them.

Since the love of money is the root of all
evil, may we not love it.

Give us a desire to do all things
for love of You.

Give us this day our daily bread, which includes
love, joy and peace, which can only come
from You, our Father.

As You are our Father, let us live as members
of one family.

Enrich our homes with the joy that comes
    from loving one another.

Turn the hearts of parents to children and the
    hearts of children to parents.

We bless You for the love of friends in heaven
    and on earth.

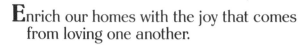

Deepen our affections.

May we walk in the light as You are in the light.

Father, we thank You for the comfort received
    from the Holy Spirit.

Fill us with Your love that we may do nothing
    that displeases You.

Help us to tell others of Your love.

The simple heart that freely asks in love, receives.

He prays best who loves best.

May we love enough to pray.

Lord,
give us
joy

Prayer is the soul's purest joy.

Lord of all joy,
Unto whom all hearts are open, all desires known,
may we declare Your works with rejoicing.

The earth is full of Your riches.

May we be happy, may we be glad, for the joy
that comes from You is our strength.

Weeping may endure for a night, but joy comes
in the morning.

May I pass this day in gladness.

Thank You for teaching me that it is more
blessed to give than to receive.

Thank You for never leaving me,
never forsaking me.

Thank You for giving me the desires of my heart.

Thank You for giving me even more than I pray for.

Thank You for this day in which to rejoice and be glad.

Thank You for giving me richly all things to enjoy.

Thank You for the joy that You have put in my heart.

Help us to do today's work well.

Bless all who work with their hands.

Give us a fervent spirit.

May we meet the anxieties of our lives with cheerfulness.

May we never forget to turn to You in our grief.

May we share our neighbors' sorrows as well
    as their joys.

May we never be deaf to Your voice or blind
    to Your light.

If we seek You, Father, we shall not lack
    any good thing.

You are our strength and our shield.

Make us glad to help in Your work,
    so that all people may learn Your love and share
    the joy that comes through Jesus Christ.

Give us true freedom.

May we give and give cheerfully.

May we in everything give thanks.

We know our labor for You is not in vain.

May we glory in our infirmities, that Your
    power may rest upon us.

May good learning flourish.

Father, from whom alone comes all true joy,
  keep my heart fixed on You.

May we delight to do Your will.

Open my eyes to the beauty all around.

Help me to make known Your mighty acts.

Many, O Lord our God, are Your wonderful works.

You are the King of all the earth. You are
  the Lord, and there is none else.

The sea is Yours, and You made it.

The day is Yours, the night also is Yours.

You have made summer and winter.

Father, it is Your pleasure to give us
  Your kindgom!

You reign, O Lord; let the earth rejoice!

Lord,
give us
peace

Give us Your peace, Father, and our hearts
shall not be troubled.

Jesus, You told us not to be afraid.

May Your peace forever rule in my heart.

You are my refuge and strength, a very present
help in trouble.

You are our hiding place; You shall preserve
us from trouble.

You have promised to keep us in perfect
peace if our minds are stayed on You.

God of hope, fill us with all joy and peace
in believing that we may abound in hope.

You are not the author of confusion,
but of peace.

May we seek peace and pursue it.

You make even our enemies to be at peace with us.

Give me wisdom, for her paths are peace.

Grant me Your peace in my sorrows.

God of all comfort, who comforts us, may
we be able to comfort those who are
in any trouble.

May we be still and know that You are God!

Except You build my house, Lord, I work
in vain.

Except You keep my city, Lord, the watchmen
wake in vain.

My safety comes from You.

I will lay down in peace and sleep.
You make me to dwell in safety.

Be my refuge, Lord, and my castle.

Father, You know our sorrows—comfort us
  in our loss and loneliness.

O God, keep us peaceful through all trouble.

Deliver me from despair and self-pity.

May I fear nothing but the loss of You.

Be the guardian of my daily life.

Teach me to try to live peaceably
  with all persons.

Help us to be of one accord and of one mind.

May we endeavor to find Your Spirit in the
  bond of peace.

We pray for all in authority, so that we may
  lead a quiet and peaceable life.

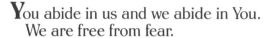You abide in us and we abide in You.
We are free from fear.

May I pass this day in peace.

Thank You, Father, for making the storm calm
so that the waves are stilled.

Bless us and keep us. Make Your face to
shine upon us and be gracious unto us.
Lift up Your countenance upon us,
and give us peace.

You give us,
Your beloved, sleep!
Thanks.

Your Word, O Lord, is a lamp unto our feet.
From the Bible we receive comfort and hope.

Underneath are Your everlasting arms.

In the multitude of my thought, Your
comforts delight my soul.

The secret of peace: the constant referral
of all anxieties to God.

None but God can satisfy the longings
of the immortal soul.

Your peace, which passes all understanding
(and all misunderstanding), shall keep
our hearts and minds through Christ Jesus.

May our peace be as a river and our righteousness as the waves of the sea.

May our hearts keep Your commandments.

If we draw near to You, You will draw near to us.

Lord,
teach us
patience

Patience is hoping, waiting, watching, praying.

Patience is the very soul of peace.

Patience is genius.

Give us the power of patience.
   When we are weak, with patience we can
   become strong. When strong, without patience
   we can become very, very weak.

If we hope for that which we see not,
   then do we with patience wait for it, Father.

If we wait and are of good courage, You have
   promised to strengthen our hearts.

May we ever rejoice in hope.

May we be patient in tribulation.

May we continue constant in prayer.

We wait for You, Lord, and in Your Word
we hope.

It is good that we should both hope and
quietly wait for Your salvation.

Give us patience with one another.

You are so patient with us, Lord.
Help us to be patient with others and
patient with ourselves.

May we daily be patient in little annoyances.
Then, when threatened by a great temptation,
we can escape by the door of patience.

Forgive us for not seeing with our eyes,
or hearing with our ears,
or understanding with our hearts.

Teach us to daily bear and forbear.

Your grace is sufficient for us;
Your strength is made perfect in weakness.
Therefore we take pleasure in infirmities, in
reproaches, in necessities, in persecutions,
in distresses for Christ's sake.

May we patiently endure so that we may obtain
the promise.

Our strength is in waiting.

Make us aware that we suffer more from our
grief and anger than from the things that grieve
and anger us.

Father, thank You for all the discipline
in life, for the tasks and trials
that teach patience.

In the shadow of Your wings will I make my refuge
until these calamities be past.

Though I walk in the midst of trouble, You will
   revive me.

Father, if this cup may not pass away from me,
   Your will be done.

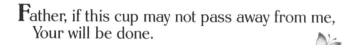

Tribulation works patience; and patience,
   experience; and experience, hope.

Order my days according to Your divine will.

Thank You for the promise that all things
   work together for good to those
   who love You.

May we be transformed by the renewing of
   our minds.

I know the world passes away.
   May I do Your will and abide forever.

May I not be unwise.
   May I understand what Your will is,
   O Lord.

Stir my will to work until Your will is done
   on earth, as it is in heaven.

Order my day according to Your divine will.

In due season we shall reap, if we faint not.

Through the comfort of the scriptures,
   may we find hope.

I will hope continually, and will praise
   You more and more.

You are dealing with us as a father deals
   with the child in whom he delights.

May You never let go of our hand when
   we stumble.

Sometimes, Lord, You wait so that You
   may be gracious unto us.
   We are blessed if we wait for You.

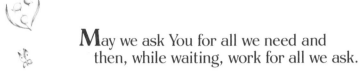

May we ask You for all we need and
   then, while waiting, work for all we ask.

You, Lord, shall renew our strength.
   We shall mount up with wings as eagles;
   we shall run and not be weary;
   we shall walk, and not faint.

Give us daily bread
   to fill our hungry body and soul.

With You as our constant friend, we can overcome the trials and temptations of this day.

Help us to seek You with our whole heart
   so that we may find You.

How rich we are if we have patience.
How poor we are if we don't.

May we run with patience this race of life.

Grant that I may run a straight race
   and not be weary.

Help me to walk in the way that I would have my children walk.

Give me strength, O Christ.

Make us patient in hard times, thoughtful in good times, and give us faith for the future.

Give us understanding, so that we may be able to withstand.

Help me to hang in there, Lord.

May we hold on and hold fast, for Your delays are never denials.

May I hold fast that which is good.

Doing Your will often means patiently waiting. Help me.

Patience is the art of hoping.

Lord,
teach us
goodness

Goodness is love in action.

The earth is full of the goodness
of You, our God!

Oh, how great is Your goodness.

You have promised that while the earth
remains, seedtime and harvest, cold and
heat, summer and winter, and day and
night shall not cease.

You are good and ready to forgive.

Father, You are good to all who wait for You
and to the soul who seeks You.

We know, Father, that goodness is not what
we do, but what we are.

May we follow the path of the just.

We pray, "Lead us not into temptation,"
for we know how weak we are.

Help me not only to resist evil, but give me
strength to depart from evil.

Send Your angels to keep me
and protect me from evil.

Search me, O God, and know my heart:
try me and know my thoughts.

Grant me Your grace. Keep me from falling.

Deliver us from a proud look and a lying tongue.
May we not sow discord among our brothers.

Deliver me from apathy.

Deliver me from resentment.

Deliver me from suspicion.

Deliver me from jealousy.

Deliver me from depression.

Deliver me from fear.

Deliver me from pride.

Deliver me from arrogance.

Deliver me from greed.

Deliver me from prejudice.

Deliver me from envy.

Deliver me from family strife.

Deliver me from hardness of heart.

Open our eyes, turn us from darkness to
light, from the power of Satan unto You.

May we confess our faults one to another
and pray one for another.

Make us honest—otherwise we pray in vain.

May we be quick to sympathize with those
who are in trouble.

We have neglected visiting
our parents, our relatives, our friends.
Forgive us, Lord.

We forget all about You and are indifferent
to our neighbor. Forgive us, Lord.

May we seek to give love, joy, and peace.

Help me to keep Your commandments, O Lord.

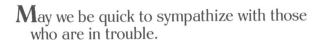

May I worship only You.

May I have no other gods before You.

Help me to take not Your Name in vain.

May I keep the Sabbath day holy.

Help me to honor my father and my mother.

May I not steal, kill or commit adultery.

May I not bear false witness against my
   neighbor or covet anything that is my neighbor's.

May I bear another's burdens and so fulfill
   the law of Christ.

Come, Holy Spirit, in all your power and
   might. Come in Your own gentle way.

Thank You, Jesus,
   for giving Yourself for our sins.

Give us the power to control our tongues
   and our lips, so that they speak no evil.

Help us to do Your will.

Teach us to do the things that You say.

Open our ears so that we may hear.
  Open our eyes so that we may see
  our opportunities to do good.

Lord, revive Your Church, beginning with us.

Help me to be my best today.

May we serve You, Lord,
  even if with bent or broken tools.

May we feed the hungry, give drink to the
  thirsty, clothe the naked. Then shall we call
  and You will answer.

May we defend the poor and orphans.

May we neglect not to visit the sick and
  those in prison.

May we ever be aware of our opportunities
to do good. Father, put us always in remem-
brance of these things. Though we know them, we
seem not to remember them at the right time.

May we never forget the truth is
forever truth and right is forever right.

We know, Father, that Your righteousness is
available to all who believe.

Help us to be rich in good works.

May we glory only in You, Lord.

May we show forth Your goodness
not only with our lips, but in our lives.

Fill us so full of Your goodness, Father,
that a bit will splash out on
every person we meet!

You have not turned away our prayers.

You have heard the voice of our supplications.

You sent Your angel to deliver us.

You heard us, and delivered us
from all our fears.

You preserve us from all evil:
You preserve our souls.

You preserve our going out and our coming in, from this time forth and even
forevermore.

Lord,
teach us
kindness

A kind soul is a river of gladness.

Father, You feed Your flock like a shepherd.
    You gather the lambs with Your arm.
    Lead us gently Father.

How gentle are Your commands!

How excellent is Your loving-kindness, O God.

Help me to show forth Your loving-kindness
    in the morning and Your faithfulness every night.

Thank You for bearing our burdens.

Fill me with Your kindness, Lord.

May we be kind to each other as You, Lord,
    are kind to us.

Give us sympathy with all who suffer wrong.

Help us to do to others as we wish
they would do to us.

May we speak kind words, for then
we shall hear kind echoes.

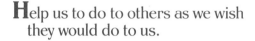

Remind me that a gentle word may soothe
some heart and banish some pain.

Any kindness, Lord, that we show is a
simple expression of Your love.

May we not forget that the
kindest thing we can do for ourselves
is to be kind to others.

Make us eager to help.

May we increase the joy of life for all of
our neighbors.

May we be tenderhearted, forgiving one another.

And may we learn to be gentle and kind
to ourselves.

Help me to be friendly and thoughtful to others.

Let me not be unkind in silence.

May I always speak gently and let no
harsh words mar any good I may do.

Help me to be especially kind to those who
spend so much of their lives with me.

Help me to remember kindnesses shown to me as
easily as I recall offenses.

Help me, Jesus, to share my neighbor's grief.

May I give kind looks, kind words and kind acts.

May we do all we can to make life less difficult
for those who live around us.

As we grow in age,
may we grow in grace and kindliness.

You have shown such kindly judgment
to our failings, Lord!

Lord,
teach us
temperance

Those who know God are humble.

Father, we know You can do everything.

We seek You, Lord, and Your strength.

Strip us of ourselves and give us Yourself.

Our help is in the name of the Lord.

We have no help but Yours, God, nor do we need
another arm save Yours to lean upon.

May we render to Caesar the things
that are Caesar's and to You the things
that are Yours.

We give thanks for those in authority.

Teach us that submission to You heals all wounds.

Help us to deny ourselves, to take up our cross
daily and follow You.

We rejoice and are glad in You.

May we remember that the fewer words
the better prayer.

Though You be high, Lord, You have respect
for the lowly.

Jesus, You are meek and lowly in heart.

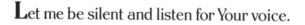

Jesus, You humbled Yourself on the cross.
May we humble ourselves in Your sight.

Help me to follow You.

Show me Your purpose for my life.

Let me be silent and listen for Your voice.

We brought nothing into this world, and it is
certain that we shall carry nothing out.

May we never boast of tomorrow, for we know
not what a day may bring.

May we say that if You will it we shall do this or that.

May we never love the praise of men more
than the praise of You.

Freely we have received.

There is no power but You.

When we stand, may we take heed lest we fall.

Help me to cast out the beam in my eye.

Keep me humble, Lord.

Let me esteem others better than myself.

You are the very Lord of the universe.
    You are King of kings and Lord of lords. To You
    belong all might and majesty.

May I be strong in You and in the power
    of Your might.

Your understanding is infinite.

You laid the foundations of the earth, and the
    heavens are the work of Your hands.

You are God, who made heaven and earth
    and the sea and all that is in them.

You have established the world by Your wisdom.

There is no searching of Your understanding.

You give power to the faint,
    and for those who have no might,
    You increase their strength.

You still the noise of the seas and the
    tumult of the people.

You tell the number of the stars;
   You call them all by name.

God, there is nothing too hard for You.

You rule by Your power forever.

May Your spirit direct and rule my heart in all
   things, at all times.

May I bear the infirmity of my brother.

Let the words of my mouth and the meditations of
   my heart be acceptable, O Lord.

Unto You, Father, I lift up my eyes. In Your light
   shall I see light.

Keep me ever in the simplicity that is in Christ.

Lord,
teach us
meekness

He who is master of himself is great.

Remind us, Lord, that he who cannot command himself is not free.

If the Son makes us free, we are free indeed!

May we offend not in words.

We know we cannot tame our tongue without Your help, Father.

May we not use proud speech.

May we not speak evil of another.

Lord, enable me to think or say nothing which may injure my neighbor.

Order my conversation aright.

Jesus, May I never deny You before others.

May I give You glory.

Help me to glorify You in my body and in my spirit, which are Yours.

Help me to speak of the glory of Your kingdom.

Help me to be master of myself, so that I may be a servant of Yours.

Imbue me daily with the competency of Your wisdom.

May we walk worthy of You, our God, who has called us into Your kingdom.

Lord,
teach us
faith

Faith is to believe what we do not see.
   Faith's reward is to see and enjoy
   what we believe.

Father, You have given to everyone a measure of
   faith. Thank You for this precious gift.

Faith is the victory that overcomes the world.

May I diligently seek You through the study of
   Your Word.

Day by day, guide me to see You in Your Word.

Faith comes by hearing Your Word.

Show me great and mighty things that I know not.

God of hope, fill me with joy in believing.

Knowing that I cannot be justified by works,
give me faith.

Help me to meditate on Your Word daily, for the
holy scriptures are able to make us wise.

Thank You, Lord, for the sign:
A virgin conceived and bore a Son, and
called His name Immanuel.

May we not stray from You, Jesus, for You are
the way.

May we not doubt You, Jesus, for You are
the truth.

Teach us to trust You.

There is neither Jew nor Greek, there is neither
bond nor free, there is neither male nor female.
We are all children of God by faith in Jesus.

Oh, for a world at unity with itself.

Thank You, Father, for giving us Your Spirit to
bear witness that we are Your children.

You have chosen the poor of this world, rich in
faith, as heirs of Your kingdom.

Give me strength so that I may earnestly contend
for the faith.

Give me grace to follow day by day in the steps
of Jesus.

Show me Your ways, O Lord.
Teach me Your paths.
Lead me in Your truth.

For unto us a Child is born, unto us a Son is
given. Thank You.

You are our God forever and ever. You will be our guide even until death.

Help me to understand that the gospel of Christ is the power of salvation to everyone who believes it.

If we believe that Jesus is the Christ, we are born of God.

If we are born again, we can overcome the world.

The victory that overcomes the world is our faith.

No one can lay any other foundation.

We know, Father, that we are saved through faith, which is a gift from You.

Jesus, You are the living bread that came down from heaven. Give us this bread.

Jesus, You are the door. I knock.

If we believe in the Son we have everlasting life.

O God, You have exalted Jesus and have given
Him a Name which is above every name. Every
knee should bow, and every tongue should
confess that Jesus Christ is Lord.

Help me to confess Jesus, as my Lord, and to
believe in my heart that He is raised from the
dead.

We walk by faith, not by sight.

Thank You for Your abiding presence,
for Your strength which is always sufficient.

Thank You for the faith that with You
nothing shall be impossible.

Help me to abide in You. Abide in me.

The end of faith is the salvation of souls.

Give me the shield of faith.

We are fellow citizens with the saints and of
    the household of God. Praise God.

May the grace of our Lord Jesus Christ,
    and the love of God, and the communion of the
    Holy Spirit be with us all.

We want more love, more peace, more patience,
    more joy, more faith, more kindness each day
    until we see You face to face.

I will cast all care upon You, for You care for me.

Help me to add virtue to my faith.

When we find no joy around us, give us Your joy.

Give us faith to believe that we shall receive when we ask.

You hear our prayers without words.

Give us confidence in You, Father.

May we trust in Your power to heal.

Heal us, O Lord, and we shall be healed. Save us and we shall be saved.

You, Lord, are my rock, and my fortress.

I will trust in Your mercy and rejoice in Your salvation.

Help me, Lord, to confess my faults to another.

Help me, Lord, to pray for another.

Father, do not let me cast away my confidence.

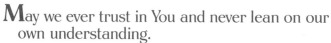

May we ever trust in You and never lean on our own understanding.

The reward for believing is great.

Thine, O Lord, is the greatness, and the power, and the glory, and the victory, and the majesty: for all that is in the heaven and in the earth is Thine; Thine is the kingdom, O Lord, and Thou art exalted as head above all.

Thank You, Jesus, for preparing us a place, so that we will be where You are.

You, Lord, have prepared Your throne in the heavens.

Your kingdom is everlasting and Your dominion endures throughout all generations.

O Lord, rule my life completely.

You will give a crown of righteousness
  to all those who love You.

Give us the water that shall be in us a wellspring
  of everlasting life.

We look toward the day of Christ's coming.

You, Lord, will come again. You died so that we
  may live.

When Christ shall appear, then shall we also
  appear with Him in glory.

That day will come when the lofty looks of man
  shall be humbled and the Lord alone shall be
  exalted. Lord, keep us humble.

Help us to be always ready.

We commit ourselves unto You, knowing You are able to keep us. We give You glory forever and ever.

Help me to spread this gospel of the kingdom in all the world. Then shall Your kingdom come.

When I am poor in spirit, Lord, help me to remember that mine is the kingdom of heaven.

Let me be born again so that I may see Your Kingdom.

Let me become as a little child, so that I may enter into heaven.

Dear Lord, may we have a share in bringing in the kingdom.

I know the glory to come will far outweigh the sufferings I now endure.

All power is given unto You, Jesus, in heaven and on earth. We praise you.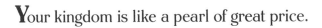

Thank You, Jesus, for going to prepare a place for me in my Father's house.

Your kingdom is like a grain of mustard seed that grew to a great tree.

Your kingdom is like leaven.

Your kingdom is like a pearl of great price.

Teach us, Lord, to observe Your kingdom within us.

Your kingdom come.

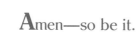

Amen—so be it.

When we pray, we believe You hear us, Father,
and we say Amen.

Our Amen is evidence that our prayers are from
our heart.

As our Amen is sincere, so is our prayer.

Even so—
Come, Lord Jesus.

Book design by John DiLorenzo
Cover and interior art by Peter Church
Typeset in EXPERT